Bond

10 Minute Tests

10-11 years

Sarah Lindsay

English

Nelson Thornes

a Wolters Kluwer business

90%

Rewrite these sentences changing them from *plural* to *singular*.

1 The leaves fell from the trees.

The leaf fell from the tree ✓

2 The children played with two skipping ropes and some footballs.

The child played a skipping rope and ✓
a football.

3 While playing, the kittens knocked the bags to the floor.

While playing, the kitten knocked the bag. ✓
to the floor

4 The swings broke and injured many children.

The swing broke and injured a child ✓

Change each of the *nouns* in **bold** to the *infinitive* of the *verb*.

5 Amil needed more practice with his **division**. to ___divide___ ✓

6 A **statement** was read out by the lawyer. to ___State___ ✓

7 The **infection** had spread to Ella's ears. to ___infect___ ✓

8 The burglar was caught by the **detective**. to ___detect___ ✓

Write an *antonym* for each of these words by adding a *prefix*.

9 happy ___unhappy___ ✓   **12** correct ___uncorrect___ ✗ w

10 frost ___unfrost___ ✗   **13** clean ___unclean___ ✓

11 grateful ___ungrateful___ ✓   **14** advantage ___unadvantage___ ✗

Complete the following proverbs.

15 Too many cooks _spoil the broth_ ✓.

16 The grass is always greener _on the other side_ ✓.

17 _When the cat is away_ ✓ the mice will play. ✓

18 _every cloud_ has a silver lining. ✓

19 The early bird _catches the worm_ ✓.

Write 'there', 'their' or 'they're' in the gap.

20 The children collected _their_ bags before going home. ✓

21–22 James and Sarah love _their_ dog and _they're_ always taking ✓
       him on long walks. _their_

23 _There_ is never enough money collected to help look after the homeless. ✓

Complete these word sums. Watch out for the spelling changes!

24 busy + ly = _busily_ ✓

25 argue + ment = _argument_ ✓

26 laugh + ing = _laughing_ ✓

27 notice + able = _noticeable_ ✓

28 complete + ly = _completely_ ✓

29 imagine + ary = _imaginary_ ✓

30 meaning + less = _meaningless_ ✓

$\frac{29 \times 10^p}{30}$ 97%

(3)

Total ▢

TEST 2: **Spelling**

Write each of these words correctly.

1	unecessary	~~unessesary~~ ~~unees~~ unnecessary	
2	libary	~~libarary~~ library	✓
3	recomend	reccomend	✓
4	qarter	quarter	✓
5	jewellry	~~jewell~~ jewellery	✓
6	diffrent	different	✓
7	buisness	~~buisness~~ ✗ business	
8	enviroment	environment	✓
9	invovled	envovled	✗
10	charcter	character	✓

Add a *prefix* to each of these to make a new word.

11	behave	missbehave	✗ ✓
12	charge	discharge	✓
13	cycle	bycycle	✗
14	mobile	~~immotete~~ immobile	✗
15	ready	unready · al	✓
16	fortune	misfortune	✓
17	angle	triangle	✓
18	continue	uncontinue	✓
19	avoidable	unaviodable	✓
20	like	dislike	✓

4

Write the *plural* forms of these words.

21 church   Churches ✓

22 waltz   ✗ waltzes ✗

23 bush   bushes ✓

24 pencil   Pencils ✓

25 wife   wivef Wives ✓

Add ie or ei to each of these to make a word.

26 br i e f ✓   30 f e i nt ✓

27 sl e i gh ✓   31 s ie ge ✓

28 ei ghty *eighty* ✓   32 r e i gn ✓

29 f i e rce ✓   33 c e i ling ✓

Each of these words has a missing silent letter. Rewrite each word correctly.

34 nockout   knockout ✓

35 colum   column ✓

36 miniture   miniature ✓

37 salm   salmn ✓ salam ✗   Psalm

38 nat   knat ✗

39 climer   climber ✓

40 nome   gnome ✓

$\frac{3.8}{40}$ 95%   (5)   Total

Nat and the Great Bath Climb   *by Penelope Lively*

Wood-lice colonies are governed by Chief Wood-lice, who are stern and ancient creatures with whiskers of immense length. Young wood-lice are kept under the most strict control by their elders; indeed they are quite literally trampled on until large enough to hold their own. Wood-lice are not creatures who go in much for expressing themselves or being original or striking out; one wood-louse acts and thinks much like another and this is the way the old wood-lice want to keep it.

From time to time the Chief Wood-louse would call the whole colony together for a meeting. The object of this meeting was for the Chief Wood-louse to lecture the newest generation of young wood-lice, who were allowed to attend as soon as their whiskers were three millimetres long, which meant they were grown-up.

The hero of this story, who was called Nat, came to his first such meeting when he was three weeks old – which in human terms is about eighteen years. The young wood-lice sat in a row at the front, feeling important but nervous, while their parents and aunts and uncles crowded behind them and the Chief Wood-louse took up a position in front.

The Chief Wood-louse looked sternly down at the **assembled** crowd and began to speak. "We are gathered together today," he said, "to remind ourselves of the purpose of life." He glared at the young wood-lice. "And what is the purpose of life?" The young wood-lice, who knew they were not supposed to answer, gazed at him respectfully.

"The purpose of life is to climb up the side of the bath. That is what we are here for. That is why we were born. No one has ever succeeded. But the purpose of life is to try. Each and every one of us. Your turn has now come. Your mothers and fathers have tried before you. Some brave spirits have tried several times. All have failed."

There was silence. The young wood-lice gazed at the Chief Wood-louse and felt even more nervous and important. All except Nat, who was the youngest and smallest and had been in trouble most of his life for asking too many questions. Nat was thinking.

"You will make your attempts turn and turn about, starting with the eldest. Each of you will fail, but will have made a glorious attempt, you will then have your names inscribed on the Roll of Honour."

The young wood-lice went quite pink with pride and excitement, all except Nat, who raised one of his fourteen legs. "Please, sir," he said, "why do we have to climb up the side of the bath?"

There was a gasp of horror from the crowd of wood-lice. Nat's mother fainted clean away; his father bent his head in shame.

The Chief Wood-louse stared at Nat. His whiskers twitched in fury. "WHAT DID YOU SAY?"

Nat cleared his throat and repeated, politely and clearly, "Why do we have to climb up the side of the bath?"

The Chief Wood-louse huffed and puffed; his little black eyes bulged; **he creaked with indignation**. "BECAUSE IT'S THERE!" he roared…

Answer these questions about the extract.

1 Who controls young wood-lice?

The elders

2 Write a sentence describing what wood-lice elders are like.

They are strict. Elder wood lice are strict.

3 How long do wood-lice whiskers have to be before wood-lice are considered to be grown-up?

3 millimeters long

4 How do you think the parents of the young wood-lice felt, waiting for the Chief Wood-louse to begin the meeting?

I think they felt nervous and proud

5 What is the meeting for?

To remind wood lice the purpose of life climbing up the Bath

6 Why had Nat been in trouble for most of his life?

He kept on asking questions

7 Why were all the wood-lice shocked when Nat asked a question?

Because it has no answer

8 What do you think happened next?

He got really angry and he never climbed up the bath

9 What does the word 'assembled' mean? *gathered*

10 What is meant by 'he creaked with indignation'?

he said it in anger

7

Total

Add to each of these words to make a *compound word*.

1 sun _____ Sh~ Sunshine ✓

2 hand _____ handshake ✓

3 snow _____ snowball or snow board ✓

4 pen _____ Pen friend ✓

5 light _____ light weight ✓

6 trap _____ trap door ✓

7 foot _____ football ✓

8 rain _____ rain bow ✓

Change these sentences into *reported speech*.

9 "If we don't hurry we'll be late," shouted Zoe.

_____ Zoe shouted if we don't hurry we'll be late

10 Beth enquired, "Is this the way to the toilets?"

_____ is this the way to the toilets enquired Beth ✗

11 "Quick, the guard dog is catching us!" screamed Dan.

_____ Dan screamed wick the quick the guard dog is catching us ✓

12 "What time is it?" asked Mrs Sparks.

_____ Mrs Sparks asked what ts the time ✓

13 Mum whispered, "Remember, when you wake up in the morning it will be your birthday!"

_____ Remember when you wake up in the morning it will be you Birthday whispered mum

Write a *homophone* for each of these words.

14	cereal	Serial ✓	19	heard	herd ✓
15	great	grate ✓	20	wait	weight ✓
16	horse	hoarse ✓	21	piece	peace
17	bough	bow ✓	22	sent	scent ✓
18	beach	beech ✓			

Punctuate this passage correctly. Remember to start a new line when it is needed.

23–40   Class 6 was having a swimming lesson I'm exhausted exclaimed Eva I wish something more exciting would happen I agree because if I do one more length of this pool I'll scream moaned Lee Suddenly Eva's wish came true as Mrs Davey their teacher slipped on some water at the side of the pool She fell headfirst into the pool

Class 6 was having a swimming
lesson "I'm exhausted" exclaimed Eva "I wish
something more exting would happen". I agree
because if I do one more length of this
pool I'll scream" moaned Lee". Suddenly
Eva's wish came true as mrs Davey
thier teacher Slipped on some water at
the side of the pool. She fell headfirst
into the pool

TEST 5: **Vocabulary**

Test time: 0 | | | | | 5 | | | | | 10 minutes

Write these words in *alphabetical order*.

thrush   thunderstorm   thread   throat   thumb

1 *thread*

2 *throat*

3 *thrush*

4 *thumb*

5 *thunderstorm*

Write six *synonyms* for the word 'said'.

6 *cried*

7 *replyed*

8 *exclaimed*

9 *shouted*

10 *laughed*

11 *thought*

Write a *definition* for each of the underlined *idioms*.

12 James felt <u>over the moon</u> when he won the trophy.

Over the moon means someone is very happy

13 Meena was feeling <u>under the weather</u> having eaten five bags of crisps.

under the weather means a bit unwell

14 Ben had <u>a change of heart</u>; he didn't want to play outside in the rain!

a change of heart means, he changed his mind

(10)

Write a *definition* for each of these words.

15 ponder _To think clearly about something_

16 unmistakable _always right_

17 cooperate _do stuff with eachother_

18 occupation _What is yours th Job_

19 percentage _Out of a hundred_

20 submerge _Join into_

Circle the *diminutives*.

21–25   (duckling)   (calf)   (piglet)

(eaglet)   (bullock)   fawn

lamb   (owlet)   foal

Complete each sentence as a *simile*.

26 Aimee's bed was as warm as _hot Sunshine toast_.

27 Jacob ran as fast as _a Cheetah_.

28 The custard was as thick as _Cement_.

29 Jess felt as cold as _Snow_.

30 Tom's bruise was as big as _apple_.

Total [   ]

Test time: 0 |||||5|||||10 minutes

Circle the silent letter in each of these words.

1 guilt

2 knuckle

3 rhombus

4 island

5 gnat

6 crescent

7 crumb

8 answer

What are the following: commands, questions or statements?

9 Put your homework on the table _____ question

10 What time is our appointment _____ question

11 Global warming is a serious problem _____ statement

12 It's six o'clock _____ command statement

13 Where have I put my recorder _____ question

14 Sit quietly _____ command

Add the missing apostrophes.

15–16 Ill run and get my coat from Henrys house.

17 Wheres my hat?

18 Isnt it time the cinema doors opened?

Write four words used in English but derived from another language.
e.g. croissant

19 ___Dobh Dobi___

20 ___Quassel___

21 ___Madam___

22 ___Paper___

What parts of speech are each of these words?

23 after ___proposition___

24 scream ___Verb___

25 he ___Pronoun___

26 tarantula ___Noun___

27 frantically ___proposition adverb___

Write a *definition* for each of these words in as few words as possible.

28 permanent

___Something that stays forever long___

29 pursue

___chase___

30 particle

___a part of something___

Test time: 0 _|_|_|_|_|_5_|_|_|_|_10 minutes

Write two examples of each of the following.

1–2 common nouns _____book_____ _____cat_____

3–4 abstract nouns _____air_____ _____oxegen_____

5–6 proper nouns _____God_____ _____London Vancouver_____

7–8 collective nouns _____Class_____ _____herd_____

Fill each gap with an *adverb*.

9 Matthew looked _____jealosly_____ at the sweets.

10 Hannah copied her story _____thoughtfully_____.

11 The Gallop family _____sadly_____ waved goodbye to their cousins.

12 Jacob _____unhappily_____ tidied his messy room.

Write two *adjectives* to describe each of these *nouns*.

13–14 _____shining_____ , _____blonde_____ hair

15–16 a _____growling_____ , _____ferocious_____ lion

17–18 a _____colourful_____ , _____beautiful_____ butterfly

19–20 a _____sweet_____ , _____scented_____ tree

Underline the *preposition* in each sentence.

21 Shall we meet after breakfast?

22 Jessica's cat slept on her bed.

23 Let's see how far we can swim under the water. ✗ *under*

24 Carl jumped over the broken gate.

Write three sentences, each with a *comparative adjective* and a *conjunction*.

25–26 Billy and Ted were Racing Billy wast fastest

27–28 Jakek and Jazzy jumped from a diving board Jazzy jumped Deeper

29–30 Sound contest and Cinoma system, was loudest

Total

Read this poem carefully.

The Sands of Dee

"O Mary, go and call the cattle home,
And call the cattle home,
And call the cattle home,
Across the sands of Dee;"
The western wind was wild and dank with foam,
And all alone went she.

The western tide crept up along the sand,
And o'er and o'er the sand,
And round and round the sand,
As far as eye could see.
The rolling mist came down and hid the land:
And never home came she.

"Oh, is it weed, or fish, or floating hair –
A tress of golden hair,
A drowned maiden's hair
Above the nets at sea?
Was never salmon yet that shone so fair
Among the stakes on Dee."

They rowed her in across the rolling foam,
The cruel, crawling foam,
The cruel, hungry foam,
To her grave beside the sea:
But still the boatmen hear her call the cattle home,
Across the sands of Dee.

by Charles Kingsley

Answer these questions about the poem.

1 What was Mary asked to do?

She was sent to call the cattle home

2 When Mary set off, what was the weather like?

It was misty ~~wind~~

3 'The rolling mist came down and hid the land:'
What image does this line conjure up in your mind?

You can't even see your
~~feet~~ or the land

4 Copy the line in the poem that informs us of Mary's death.

To her grave beside the sea

5 Why do you think the sea foam is described as cruel?

because it is made by
stormy weather

6 Where was Mary buried?

beside the sea in Dee

7 Which word in the poem means damp or moist? _foam_

8 What does 'o'er' mean? _other_

9 How do you think Mary felt when she was sent out to the sands of Dee?

Scared and lonely

10 Describe how this poem makes you feel.

It makes me feel sad

Underline the correct *verb* form in each sentence.

1 When (is/<u>are</u>) we going to get to Gran's house? ✓

2 (<u>Is</u>/Are) we meeting this afternoon? ✓

3 Todd's parents (was/<u>were</u>) pleased with his progress. ✓

4 It (<u>was</u>/were) raining outside. ✓

5 Which pony (<u>is</u>/are) Jodie's? ✓

Write each of these words correctly.

6 recieve _receive_ ✓

7 preparasion _preparation_ ✓

8 atmosfere _atmosphere_ ✓

9 decission _decision_ ✓

10 Febuary _Febiuary_ ✗

11 embarras _embarass_ ✗

12 seperate _seperate_ ✗

13 margerine _margerine_ ✗

14 vegtable _vegetable_ ✓

15 resturant _resturant_ ✗

Write a short conversation between two friends discussing what they might do after school. Be careful to start new lines when they are needed and to punctuate the conversation correctly.

16–25

"Hey, do you want to go to my house after school," said Tom. "Yeh that would be great," said Ted. "What time??" asked

"What time"? asked Ted. "4:30," Said Tom.

"See you tlg!" they both shouted.

Write five *synonyms* for the word 'nice'.

26   good

27   fine

28   great

29   lovely

30   exellent

Total

TEST 10: **Sentences**

Test time: 0 — 5 — 10 minutes

Write these statements as questions.

1   The water is too deep to swim in.

Is the water too deep to swim in? ✓

2   Andy is hiding in the woods.

Is Andy hiding in the woods? ✓

3   Bola isn't allowed out on his bike.

Isn't Bola allowed out on his bike? ✓

4   My birthday is in February.

Is my birthday in February? ✓

5   It takes Sophie thirty minutes to walk to school.

Does it take Sophie thirty minutes to walk to
School ✓

Write two sentences. Each sentence needs to have two commas.

6–7   _The cat was fat, shiny, fury and silky._ ✓

8–9   _How old is Sophie, Bill, Ted, and Fred._ ✓

Rewrite this short passage correctly. Remember to begin a new line when a different person starts to speak.

10–20 Is it Gym Club tonight asked Thomas It always is on Monday replied Poppy Thomas groaned he'd forgotten his PE kit again

"Is it Gym Club tonight" asked Thomas.
"It always is on monday" replied poppy.
Thomas groaned. He'd forgotten his PE
kit again.

Rewrite these sentences without double negatives.

21 We didn't want no homework.

_____

22 Jake hasn't no problem learning his spellings.

_____

23 Dad couldn't find no gap in which to park his car.

_____

24 Mia didn't wear no coat to the disco.

_____

25 We hadn't no problem hanging up the high decorations.

_____

Total

Test time: 0 | | | | | | 5 | | | | | 10 minutes

Draw lines to link each old word with the modern word.

1   saith   are

2   remaineth   here

3   hither   says

4   abides   remain

5   art   lives

Complete each sentence with a *phrase* or *clause*.

6   Miss James _____ Patiently _____

    _____ waited for the class to listen.

7   The cat _____ qwietly _____

    _____ pounced on its prey.

8   Todd's computer _____ Is in Such a _____

    _____ State that it _____ frequently broke down.

9   The policeman _____ often _____

    _____ kept an eye on the man.

10 The sun _____ was burning, so hot _____

    _____ that it _____ melted the ice cream in minutes.

Write two words using each of these *prefixes*.

11–12	bi	_bicycle_	_bipedlel_
13–14	non	_non-advantage_	_non-stickable_
15–16	auto	_auto Mobile_	_automatic_
17–18	sub	_substitute_	_substance_
19–20	micro	_microchip_	_microwave_

Fill each gap with an *adjective* and *noun*.

21 Sam screamed and ran from the ___ dog quickly ___.

22 Jack snuggled closely to the ___ beautiful girl ___.

23 Freda rushed towards the ___ sweetshop excitedly happily ___.

24 Joseph raced after the ___ boy fastly ___.

Add 'able' or 'ible' to complete each word.

25 charge_able_

26 irresist_ible_

27 convert_able_

28 extend_able_

29 regrett_ible_

30 avoid_able_

Write each of these words correctly.

1 relvant   _relavant_

2 traveler   _traveller_

3 twelth   _~~twleth~~ ~~twleft~~ twelfth_

4 Wenesday   _Wednesday_

5 parliment   _parliament_

6 imediately   _immediately_

7 carribbean   _Carribean_

8 potatoe   _potato_

9 independant   _indipendent_

10 excellant   _excllenent_

Add ance or ence to each of these to make a word.

11 appear_ence_   14 occurr_ance_

12 eleg_ance_   15 sil_ence_

13 radi_ence_   16 experi_ance_

Add ant or ent to each of these to make a word.

17 pleas_ent_   20 abund_ant_

18 hesit_ant_   21 stagn_ent_

19 magnific_ent_   22 transpar_ent_

Answers

Answers will vary for questions that require children to answer in their own words. Possible answers to most of these questions are given in *italics*.

Test 1: Mixed

1 The leaf fell from the tree.
2 The child played with a skipping rope and a football.
3 While playing, the kitten knocked the bag to the floor.
4 The swing broke and injured a child.
5 to divide
6 to state
7 to infect
8 to detect
9 unhappy
10 defrost
11 ungrateful
12 incorrect
13 unclean
14 disadvantage
15 Too many cooks spoil the broth.
16 The grass is always greener on the other side.
17 While the cat's away the mice will play.
18 Every cloud has a silver lining.
19 The early bird catches the worm.
20 their
21–22 their, they're
23 There
24 busily
25 argument
26 laughing
27 noticeable
28 completely
29 imaginary
30 meaningless

Test 2: Spelling

1 unnecessary
2 library
3 recommend
4 quarter
5 jewellery
6 different
7 business
8 environment
9 involved
10 character
11 *misbehave*
12 *recharge*
13 *tricycle*
14 *automobile*
15 *unready*
16 *misfortune*
17 *triangle*
18 *discontinue*
19 *unavoidable*
20 *dislike*
21 churches
22 waltzes
23 bushes
24 pencils
25 wives
26 brief
27 sleigh
28 eighty
29 fierce
30 feint
31 siege
32 reign
33 ceiling
34 **k**nockout
35 colum**n**
36 min**ia**ture
37 **p**salm
38 **g**nat
39 climbe**r**
40 **g**nome

Test 3: Comprehension

1 Young wood-lice are controlled by their elders.
2 *Wood-lice elders are strict and set in their ways.*
3 Wood-lice whiskers have to be 3 millimetres long.
4 *The parents of the young wood-lice would have felt proud that their young were attending the meeting but also probably a little nervous.*
5 The purpose of the meeting is to remind themselves of the purpose of life.
6 He was often in trouble for asking too many questions.
7 *The wood-lice were shocked because nobody ever asked the Chief Wood-louse questions.*
8 *Child's own answer*
9 *brought together*
10 *he moved with displeasure*

Test 4: Mixed

1 *sunlight*
2 *handbag*
3 *snowball*
4 *penknife*
5 *lighthouse*
6 *trapdoor*
7 *football*
8 *rainfall*
9 *Zoe shouted that if we didn't hurry we'd be late.*
10 *Beth enquired whether that was the way to the toilets.*
11 *Dan screamed that we had to be quick as the guard dog was catching us.*
12 *Mrs Sparks asked what time it was.*
13 *Mum whispered to remind me that when I woke up in the morning it would be my birthday.*
14 serial
15 grate
16 hoarse
17 bow
18 beech
19 herd
20 weight
21 peace
22 scent or cent
23–40 Class 6 was having a swimming lesson.
"I'm exhausted," exclaimed Eva. "I wish something more exciting would happen."
"I agree because if I do one more length of this pool I'll scream!" moaned Lee. Suddenly, Eva's wish came true as Mrs Davey, their teacher, slipped on some water at the side of the pool. She fell headfirst into the pool!

Test 5: Vocabulary

1 thread
2 throat
3 thrush
4 thumb
5 thunderstorm
6–11 *cried, exclaimed, laughed, replied, shouted, thought.*
12 *very pleased*
13 *sick*
14 *changed his mind*
15 *to think carefully about something*
16 *clear, obvious*
17 *to work willingly with others*
18 *a job or something to fill one's time*
19 *something divided into a hundred parts*
20 *to go under water*
21–25 duckling, piglet, eaglet, bullock, owlet
26 *toast*
27 *a cheetah*
28 *cement*
29 *ice*
30 *an apple*

TEST 6: Mixed

1	u	8	w
2	k	9	command
3	h	10	question
4	s	11	statement
5	g	12	statement
6	c	13	question
7	b	14	command

15–16 I'll run and ... Henry's house.
17 Where's my hat?
18 Isn't it time the ...
19–22 *pizza, origami, umbrella, siesta.*
23 preposition or conjunction
24 verb or noun
25 pronoun
26 noun
27 adverb
28 *something that lasts forever*
29 *to chase something*
30 *a very tiny piece or amount of something*

TEST 7: Grammar

1–2 *chair, house*
3–4 *love, beauty*
5–6 *Beth, England*
7–8 *crowd, gaggle*
9 *longingly*
10 *neatly*
11 *sadly*
12 *grumpily*
13–14 *long, black*
15–16 *large, snarling*
17–18 *small, fragile*
19–20 *tall, fruit*
21 after
22 on
23 under
24 over
25–30 *Child's own answer*

TEST 8: Comprehension

1 *Mary was asked to call the cattle home.*
2 *There was a wild wind when Mary set off.*
3 *Child's own answer*
4 *'A drowned maiden's hair'*
5 *The sea is described as cruel, as it was the sea in which Mary died.*
6 *Mary was buried beside the sea.*
7 dank
8 over
9 *Child's own answer*
10 *Child's own answer*

TEST 9: Mixed

1	are	9	decision
2	Are	10	February
3	were	11	embarrass
4	was	12	separate
5	is	13	margarine
6	receive	14	vegetable
7	preparation	15	restaurant
8	atmosphere		

16–25 *Child's own answer. Give marks for correct layout and punctuation.*
26–30 *pleasant, lovely, enjoyable, good, likeable.*

TEST 10: Sentences

1 Is the water too deep to swim in?
2 Is Andy hiding in the woods?
3 Isn't Bola allowed out on his bike?
4 Is my birthday in February?
5 Does it take Sophie thirty minutes to walk to school?
6–9 *Child's own answer*
10–20 "Is it Gym Club tonight?" asked Thomas.
"It always is on Monday," replied Poppy.
Thomas groaned. He'd forgotten his PE kit again.
21 We didn't want any homework.
22 Jake hasn't a problem learning his spellings. *or* Jake has no problem learning his spellings.
23 Dad couldn't find a gap in which to park his car. *or* Dad could find no gap in which to park his car.
24 Mia didn't wear a coat to the disco.
25 We didn't have a problem hanging up the high decorations. *or* We had no problem hanging up the high decorations.

TEST 11: Mixed

1 saith – says
2 remaineth – remain
3 hither – here
4 abides – lives
5 art – are
6–10 *Child's own answer*
11–12 *bicycle, biceps*
13–14 *non-smoker, nonsense*
15–16 *autograph, automatic*
17–18 *submarine, subscribe*
19–20 *microphone, microwave*
21 *haunted house*
22 *crackling fire*
23 *shoe shop*
24 *small dog*
25 chargeable
26 irresistible
27 convertible
28 extendable
29 regrettable
30 avoidable

TEST 12: Spelling

1	relevant	13	radiance
2	traveller	14	occurrence
3	twelfth	15	silence
4	Wednesday	16	experience
5	parliament	17	pleasant
6	immediately	18	hesitant
7	Caribbean	19	magnificent
8	potato	20	abundant
9	independent	21	stagnant
10	excellent	22	transparent
11	appearance	23	garden
12	elegance	24	ornament

25 resist
26 notice
27 shine
28 happy
29 alter
30 giraffe
31 pulley
32 grammar

33 professor
34 necessary
35 wrapping
36 running
37 organiser
38 careless
39 hiking
40 peaceful

Test 13: Comprehension

1 Pedigree dogs are the most expensive to buy.
2 Some pedigree dogs are unsuitable to keep as pets because they are traditionally bred to work.
3 A Dalmatian needs plenty of exercise.
4 It is possible to estimate the size of a cross-bred dog when both parents are known.
5 *Cross-breds are cheaper to buy, stronger in constitution and less highly strung.*
6 A mongrel dog's parents are of mixed ancestry; a mix of different dogs.
7 Some mongrels are difficult to home because it is hard to predict accurately how they will develop since their sires are unknown.
8 *Child's own answer*
9 offspring
10 sturdy

Test 14: Mixed

1 bushes
2 athletes
3 convoys
4 motifs
5 kangaroos
6 babies
7–9 *Child's own answers, e.g.*
Using **n**ew **n**apkins **e**ight **c**hildren **e**at **s**ugary **s**weets **a**nd **r**aspberry **y**oghurts.
10–11 Grandad, who was feeling grumpy anyway, got really cross ...
12–13 ... perhaps the sound of the wind howling, sirens screaming, leaves rustling ...
14 To be able to understand your

own beliefs and values, you need to ...
15–16 *friendly, friendship*
17–18 *shameful, shameless*
19–20 *happiness, happily*
21–22 *painful, painless*
23–24 *greatness, greatly*
25–30 *Child's own answer*

Test 15: Vocabulary

1–5 *Child's own sentences. Five sentences containing the listed words.*
6 husband
7 prince
8 nephew
9 gentleman
10 lion
11 fox
12–15 television, DVD player, astronaut, website
16 compact disc
17 kilogram
18 United States of America
19 South East or Stock Exchange
20 Member of Parliament
21–22 *outfit, outlaw*
23–24 *thrill, throne*
25–26 *disgrace, dispatch*
27 *The wind was a howling beast.*
28 *The snow is soft balls of cotton wool.*
29 *The leaves are a prickly carpet.*
30 *His bedroom was a tip!*

Test 16: Mixed

1–8 common noun: *man*
proper noun: *Lucy*
abstract noun: *appearance*
collective noun: *bunch*
9 "Ben, it is time to put the chips in the oven," called Mum.
10 "There's nothing to worry about," said the vet.
11 "It's time for lunch," announced Mrs Owen.
12 "Rupesh, would you like to stay the night at my house?" asked Ryan.
13 shampoo
14 shave
15 shawl
16 shelf

17 shelter
18 *The water was as blue as sapphire.*
19 *The swan was as white as snow.*
20 *The drum was as loud as a thunder clap.*
21 *Jo saw a spider that was as big as a house.*
22 *The monkey sat as quiet as a mouse.*
23 marine
24 claim
25 post
26 digest
27 rely
28 nation
29 hygiene
30 offence

Test 17: Grammar

1–2 *ran quickly*
3–4 *worked slowly*
5–6 *searched helplessly*
7–8 *sat patiently*
9–10 *talked quietly*
11–15 *child's own answer*
16 *an unusually large banana*
17 *the extremely naughty children*
18 *a scary black spider*
19 *the suprisingly calm wind*
20 *a really exciting computer game*
21–22 *friendship, hatred*
23–24 *above, under*
25–26 *(to) sit, (to) laugh*
27–28 *it, he*
29–30 *the smallest, the largest*

Test 18: Comprehension

1 The Second World War.
2 He let him win at marbles; he lent him his wicket keeper's gloves; he gave him his best stamp.
3 Everyone knew when he arrived at school with grazed knees, dirt on his blazer and red eyes from crying.
4 He believed this because the boy's father was an electrician rather than being at the front line.
5 *Child's own answer*

6 He worked in a button factory.

7 *Child's own answer*

8 *He was hiding his embarrassment about the fact that his father hadn't gone off to fight in the war.*

9 *Child's own answer*

10 Most men were going off to fight in the war, and those who died were thought of as heroes.

TEST 19: **Mixed**

1 *Two people can be more successful at doing something than one person.*

2 *You get better at something with practice.*

3 *If you help me, I will help you.*

4 *It is best not to change things.*

5–11 "Can I open my present now?" asked Gina. "I have waited a very long time!"

12–16 "Let's go ice-skating," suggested Jenny.

17–18 *crash, whoosh*

19–20 *hissing, slithering*

21–22 *whizz, fizzle*

23 pronoun

24 conjunction

25 adverb

26 verb or noun

27 verb or noun

28–30 *Child's own answers*

TEST 20: **Sentences**

1 were   4 was

2 was   5 was

3 were

6–10 *Child's own answers*

11–15 "Quieten down!" bellowed the headteacher.

16–18 Darren raced towards the ball, not wanting to be beaten by anyone.

19–23 "Are we going to win?" called Helen.

24 Dad left on a business trip to the USA this morning.

---

25 On Friday Garry is staying the night.

26 The Victorian school bell is rung every day at nine o'clock in the morning.

27 Dave's cats, Batman and Robin, tore up his Harry Potter poster.

28 The train was late, eventually arriving in Manchester after Manchester United had won their match!

Puzzle ❶

1 South Africa

2 department store

3 Downing Street

4 pencil crayon

5 shopping trolley

6 Prince William

7 swimming costume

8 Blue Peter

A and B
   Child's own answers

Puzzle ❷

necessary, innocent, receive, decision

gaol, religion, vegetable, imagination

Puzzle ❸

For example:

happy – happily, happiest, unhappy

phone – telephone, microphone, phoneme

question – questioning, questionable, questioned

detect – detective, detecting, detectable

graph – telegraph, autograph, photograph

Puzzle ❹

Child's own answers

Puzzle ❺

Across	Down
2 bicycle	1 octagon
3 triathlon	4 tripod
5 octopus	
6 decade	

Write the *root word* of each of these words.

23 gardener _____ garden _____

24 ornamental _____ ornament _____

25 resistance _____ resist _____

26 noticeable _____ notice _____

27 shiny _____ shine _____

28 happiness _____ happy _____

29 alteration _____ alter _____

Add the missing double letters to each of these words.

30 gira _ff_ e   33 profe _ss_ or

31 pu _ll_ ey   34 nece _ss_ ary

32 gra _mm_ ar   35 wra _pp_ ing

Complete these word sums. Watch out for the spelling changes!

36 run + ing = _____ running _____

37 organise + er = _____ organiser _____

38 care + less = _____ careless _____

39 hike + ing = _____ hiking _____

40 peace + ful = _____ peaceful _____

Pedigree or mongrel?

Pedigree dogs

Pedigree, or pure-bred, dogs are the most expensive to buy, but it is not usually difficult to find homes for their puppies. Being highly bred may make them more delicate than dogs of mixed ancestry and more likely to inherit defects. The very fact that they are descended from a line of dogs used traditionally for a particular form of work may make some of them unsuitable as pets for the average household. Dalmatians, for instance, were once carriage dogs. A pair of them would run alongside the horses in the capacity of outriders. Their elegant proportions and attractive, spotted coats mean they are now in demand as pets, but they should only be kept if they can be allowed plenty of exercise.

Cross-bred dogs

Cross-breds are the **progeny of two pure-bred parents** of different breeds. Cross-breds usually make very good pets. They are cheaper to buy, but of course cost as much to keep as pedigree dogs. When both parents are known, it is possible to estimate the adult size and type of cross-bred puppy. Depending on the combination of the parents' characteristics, a cross-bred dog can be very attractive, and may be stronger in constitution and often less highly strung than either of its parents.

Mongrel dogs

Mongrels are dogs of mixed ancestry. They are inexpensive and most make affectionate companions. Nearly all mongrels are **robust**, but since their sires are often unknown, it is impossible to predict accurately how mongrel puppies will develop. This is one reason why mongrels are difficult to home, and why so many are taken to animal welfare societies, such as the RSPCA, from which they can sometimes be adopted.

The Official RSPCA Pet Guide
Care for Your Dog

Answer these questions about the extract.

1 Which type of dog is most expensive to buy?

Pedigree dogs or pure breed

2 Why are some pedigree dogs unsuitable to keep as pets for the average household?

because thier ancestors were made to do work

3 If a Dalmatian is kept as a pet what does it particularly need?

excercise

4 When is it possible to estimate the adult size of a cross-bred dog?

when both parents are known

5 Write three differences between pedigree and cross-bred dogs.

Pedigree dog have the same breed parents.
Pedigree dogs ancestors were made to
work and some Pedigree dogs are unsuitable as pets

6 Describe the parents of a mongrel dog.

Mongrel dogs parents are unknown and mixed
usually

7 Why are some mongrel dogs difficult to home?

They don't know how thier puppies
will develop

8 Which type of dog would you choose to keep and why?

I would chose to keep a mongrel
dog because they are less cared for

9 What is meant by the word '**progeny**'?

I think the word progeny means
offspring

10 What does '**robust**' mean? _means ancestors are_
different

(27)

Total ☐

Test time: 0 | | | | | 5 | | | | | 10 minutes

Write each of these *nouns* in its *plural* form.

1   bush   _bushes_ ✓

2   athlete   _athletes_

3   convoy   _convoies_ ✗

4   motif   _motives_ ✓

5   kangaroo   _kangaroos_ ✓

6   baby   _babygies_

Write a *mnemonic* to help you remember how to spell each of these words.

7   February

Eat eggs buy rats, um umbrellas
and rats yeue

8   jewellery

Jack eats weed eggs, lollipops, ✓
levers, even rats yeue

9   unnecessary

umbrellas never never eat cats
eat snakes, snakes and rats yeue

Add the missing commas to these sentences.

10–11   Grandad, who was feeling grumpy, anyway, got really cross when the puppy chewed his new slippers.

12–13   Take a few moments to listen to different sounds – perhaps the sound of the wind howling, sirens screaming, leaves rustling, or buzzing planes.

14   To be able to understand your own beliefs and values, you need to learn about the beliefs and values of others.

Add two *suffixes* to each of these to make new words.

15–16	friend	friendly	friendship
17–18	shame	shameful	shameless
19–20	happy	happiness	happiness
21–22	pain	painful	painless
23–24	great	greatful	greatless

Write three sentences, each including an *adjective* and a *verb*.

25–26   I ran up to the football pitch, I could see the emerald green grass.

27–28   I jumped into the wrestling ring in the middle, I saw the gigantic arena

29–30   I played cricket, the ball was ruby red.

Total

Test 15: **Vocabulary**

Write each of these words in a sentence.

withhold

1 _"I will withold your toy untill you lern to behave" said the teacher._

access

2 _The access to the castle was through the door_

opportunity

3 _"This is a great opportunity" Said the teacher._

persistence

4 _persistence is to hold on_

mischievous

5 _The boy is mischievous_

Write the masculine gender of each of these words.

6 wife _husband_

7 princess _prince_

8 niece _nephew_

9 lady _Gentle men_

10 lioness _lion_

11 vixen _fox_

Circle the words that have come into our language in the last 100 years.

12–15

chimney   television   box

pottery   DVD player   glass   astronaut

bicycle   website   mantelpiece

Write these *abbreviations* in full.

16 CD _____Cat Disc_____ (crossed out)

17 kg _____kilo grams_____

18 USA _____United States of America_____

19 SE _____

20 MP _____Member of Parliment_____

Fill the gaps with two words. The four words in each set need to be in *alphabetical order*.

21–22 outback _____Outcast_____ _____out draft_____ outsider

23–24 thread _____ _____ thrush

25–26 disease _____ _____ distress

Write a *metaphor* for each of these subjects.

27 wind

Wind is a

The is howling beast

28 snow

snow

He is as soft as cotton wool

29 leaves

the leaves are as green as

a swamp

30 bedroom

The bedroom is a tip

Total

List the four different types of *noun*. Write an example of each.

1–2 _Paramuer_ noun   e.g. _To know_ Proper Noun

3–4 _Collection_ noun   e.g. _Collective noun_

5–6 _Woman_ noun   e.g. _Common noun_ ✓

7–8 _Appearance_ noun   e.g. _Abstract noun_ ✓

Write these sentences as *direct speech*.

9 Mum called to Ben that it was time to put the chips in the oven.

"Ben, it's time to put the chips in the oven,"
called mum.

10 The vet told me there was nothing to worry about.

"There is nothing to worry about," said the
Vet.

11 Mrs Owen announced it was time for lunch.

"It is time for lunch," announced Mrs Owen

12 Ryan asked Rupesh if he would like to stay the night at his house.

"Rupesh would you like to stay the night at
my house," asked Ryan?

Write these words in *alphabetical order*.

shave   shampoo   shawl   shelter   shelf

13 _Shampoo_

14 _Shave_

15 _Shawl_

16 _Shelf_

17 _Shelter_

Write a *simile* using the following subjects.

18 water

Water is ~~the sky sea~~ as blue as the sky.

19 swan

The swan is as white as snow.

20 drum

the drum is as loud as a roaring tiger.

21 spider

The spider is as small as a germ.

22 monkey

The monkey is as agile as a cheetah

Write the *root word* of each of these words.

23 submarine ___sub___

24 exclaim ___claim___

25 postage ___post___

26 digestible ___digest___

27 reliable ___rely___

28 international ___inter___

29 hygienic ___hygiene___

30 offensive ___offence___

Total

Add a different *verb* and *adverb* to each sentence.

1–2   Fiona _____ walked _____ quickly to the other side of the playground.

3–4   The postman _____ delivered _____ fastly _____ in the rain.

5–6   The abandoned dog _____ searched _____ sadly _____ for his home.

7–8   The bird _____ sat _____ patiently on her eggs waiting for them to hatch.

9–10   Mrs Seal's class _____ stood _____ silently _____ as they waited for lunch.

Complete these sentences. Use a *conjunction* from the box in each one.
You may use each word only once.

because	but	however	when	therefore

11   Molly loved her party dress _____ however she had _____ had it for a long time.

12   Reuben had saved his pocket money for weeks _____ because he _____ was saving up for a new bike.

13   Bill and Jake planned to meet in town _____ but it started to _____ rain.

14   The snake watched the mouse _____ when the mouse came _____ out it killed it and ate it.

15   The sheep escaped from their field _____ therefore it could _____ eat the green grass on the other side.

Write an *adjectival phrase* about each of these *nouns*.

16   a banana

A B bannana is very yellow like hay.

17   the children

The children screamed and shouted in the Playground like angry lions.

18   a spider

A Spider wove its web like a busy bee.

19   the wind

The Wind was howling like a pack of wolves

20   a computer game

A computer game was as exciting as a football match.

Write two examples of each of the following.

21–22	abstract noun	love	Compasion
23–24	preposition	on	under
25–26	verb	running	Walking
27–28	pronoun	he	She
29–30	superlative adjective	Best	worsest

Total

Hurricane Summer *by Robert Swindells*

Funny things, friendships. They tend to come and go, but most people have a special friend who stands out among all the others. I'm lucky – I've got two. One of them's been dead a long time now, but it doesn't matter – he'll always be my friend. As for the other ... well, as I said, friendships are funny. Best thing I can do is tell you about them.

The Second World War was on and I was ten. I was an only child. My dad had been killed the previous autumn serving with the Navy. Mum said I must always remember that my dad had been a hero, and I knew he had, that was the trouble.

You see, I wasn't a hero. Far from it.

There was this lad at school. Clive Simcox. He was the same age as me – we were in the same class – but Clive was taller and heavier, and for some reason that summer he started picking on me. I didn't like fighting so I was forever trying to please him. I let him win at marbles and lent him my wicket keeper's gloves. I even gave him my best stamp – a Guadeloupe triangular – but it was no use. He'd still ambush me on the way home from school and bash me up. He used to wait for me in the mornings too, and trip me as I ran past. I'd arrive at school with grazed knees and dirt on my blazer and red eyes from crying, and everybody would know Clive had had another go at me.

He used to make remarks about my Dad, which was even worse. Before the war Dad had been an electrician, so they made him an electrician in the Navy. I don't know what his work was exactly, but it had to do with electrical circuits and that sort of thing. Anyway, Clive had latched on to this and sometimes he'd say, "He **was nothing special**, you know, your dad. He wasn't a gunner or a torpedo man. He didn't kill any Germans. He was just an electrician, mending fuses and changing lightbulbs while other fellows did the fighting." This would be in the playground or on the street and he'd say it at the top of his voice so everyone could hear, and all the time he'd be pushing me – shoving me in the chest so that I had to keep stepping backwards. He was goading me of course – trying to make me fight, but I was too scared. Red-faced with shame, I'd retreat till he got bored and went off to bother somebody else.

I **despised** myself. I'd think, what sort of kid doesn't stick up for his dead father? Defend his honour? If I was half the hero Dad was, I'd stand up to Simcox and punch him on the nose, even if he bashed me up after ... When it came to it – when he was actually there in front of me with his red face and mocking eyes – I'd either try to run or let him hit me to get it over. I was ashamed of myself but I couldn't help it.

Funniest thing was, Simcox senior wasn't even in the forces. He worked in a button factory, but I daren't bring that up when Clive was tormenting me. Shows how scared I was, and believe me it's no joke being a coward when the world seems **full of heroes**.

Answer these questions about the extract.

1   In which war had the boy's father died? ___2nd world war___

2   List the three ways the boy tried to please Clive Simcox.

   ___Let him win at marbles, lent him___
   ___wicket keeper gloves and gave his___
   ___best stamp to him.___

3   How did everyone know when Clive had bullied the boy?

   ___he always made fun of him and the___
   ___other boys they were always graded___

4   Why did Clive Simcox believe the boy's father **'was nothing special'**?

   ___because he was just an electrician___

5   In your own words describe why the boy **'despised'** himself.

   ___he didn't stick up for his father or___
   ___himself.___

6   What did Clive Simcox's dad do during the war?

   ___he worked in the navy as an electrician___

7   How do you think Clive Simcox felt while bullying the boy?

   ___I think he felt he was the boss___

8   Why do you think Clive Simcox was a bully?

   ___because he was bigger than everyone___
   ___else in the school___

9   When you see someone being bullied how do you feel?

   ___If its someone I hate I don't___
   ___care if it is one of my friends___
   ___I'd help them___

10 Why did the world seem **'full of heroes'**?

   ___Because lots of people are risking their___
   ___lives at war and stuff___

Total [   ]

Write the meaning of each of these proverbs.

1 Two heads are better than one.

You should help other people because they will get better

2 Practice makes perfect.

If you want something bad keep practicing and you'll get it

3 You scratch my back and I'll scratch yours.

you help me and i'll help you

4 Let sleeping dogs lie.

let someone if someone hasn't done anything to you don't do anything to them too.

Rewrite these sentences with the missing punctuation.

5–11 Can I open my present now asked Gina I have waited a very long time

"Can I open my present now?" asked Gina "I have waited a very long time."

12–16 Lets go ice-skating suggested Jenny

"Lets go ice-skating" suggested Jenny.

Write two *onomatopoeic* words that can describe each of these.

17–18 an avalanche Crash Woosh

19–20 a snake hiss Slither

21–22 a firework bang Wee

What parts of speech are each of these words?

23 it Pronoun

24 but Conjunction

25 grumpily adjective

26 hate abstract noun

27 remove verb

Write an example of each of the following.

28 a question

How are you?

29 a statement

I go to bed. Friday. We're going to a footie match

30 a command

Go to bed

39

Total

Add 'was' or 'were' to each sentence to make it correct.

1   The Jacob family _____were_____ relieved to reach their holiday home.

2   The dog barked excitedly every time the ball _____was_____ thrown to him.

3   Mrs Trevis's children _____were_____ very well-behaved during the concert.

4   Half the audience cheered when the villain _____was_____ caught.

5   Hannah _____was_____ too excited to sleep.

Complete each sentence with a *phrase* or *clause*.

6   The horses _____eagerly and anticipately_____

_____ waited for their morning feed.

7   Ben rode his bike _____eagerly and quickly_____

_____excitedly_____ to Tuhil's house.

8   Rebecca _____Patiently_____

_____ waited for her brother.

9   The snake _____quickly and_____

_____quietly_____ escaped from its vivarium.

10 Mr Todd's class _____joyfully_____

_____ ran towards the play equipment.

Rewrite these sentences correctly.

11–15 quieten down bellowed the headteacher

"Quieten down" bellowed the Headteacher.

16–18 darren raced towards the ball not wanting to be beaten by anyone

Darren raced towards the ball not wanting to be beaten by anyone

19–23 are we going to win called Helen

"Are we going to win" called Helen.

Circle the letters in these sentences that need capitals.

24 dad left on a business trip to the usa this morning.

25 on friday, garry is staying the night.

26 the victorian school bell is rung every day at nine o'clock in the morning.

27 dave's cats, batman and robin, tore up his harry potter poster.

28 the train was late, eventually arriving in manchester after manchester united had won their match!

Puzzle ❶

In each of these groups of letters there are two words muddled together but with the letters placed in the correct order.

Can you sort the muddled words?

All capital letters are missing. Use the clues to help.

1   asfroiutcha
    (a country)
    _____   _____

2   sdtepoarrtmenet
    (a type of shop)
    _____   _____

3   dsotwrneientg
    (a place in London)
    _____   _____

4   crpeanciylon
    (can be used to mark paper)   _____   _____

5   strhooppllienyg
    (used in a supermarket)
    _____   _____

6   wprirlnlicame
    (a famous person)
    _____   _____

7   csoswitmumimnge
    *(needed when doing the
    crawl or breaststroke)*
    _____   _____

8   bpeltueer
    (a television programme)   _blue_____   _Peter_____

Write some muddled words and clues of your own.

Try them out on someone.

A   tMordwlrwseitnlgnetaintee
    _____
    (The worlds great sport and show)

B   AHSUERENMCTNTDIE
    _____
    (The word's greatest football team

Puzzle ❷

Find four soft c and four soft g words in this wordsearch.

b	k	r	e	c	e	i	v	e	v
n	d	g	n	s	t	m	d	f	e
e	g	a	o	l	f	a	c	n	g
c	x	k	c	a	k	g	o	g	e
e	r	e	l	i	g	i	o	n	t
s	a	d	b	t	s	n	b	s	a
s	f	d	n	i	d	a	d	n	b
a	n	s	c	b	s	t	n	t	l
r	c	e	t	o	z	i	m	b	e
y	d	o	g	n	d	o	c	g	a
i	n	n	o	c	e	n	t	o	k

Write the words you have found.

soft c words

_____Cent_____

_____

_____

_____

soft g words

_____

_____

_____

_____

Puzzle ❸

How many words can you find from the same word family?

spark

_____ spark**ler**

_____ spark**ling**

_____ spark**le**

_____

_____

happy

_____ unhappy

_____ happiness

_____

_____

_____

phone

_____ telephone

_____ mobile phone

_____

_____

_____

question

_____ question mark

_____

_____

_____

_____

detect

_____ detecter

_____

_____

_____

_____

graph

_____ paragraph

_____

_____

_____

_____

Puzzle 4

As time passes more and more words are being invented.

For example the word 'cheeseburger' was invented to describe a hamburger that had cheese added to it.

Invent your own words for:

a hovering skateboard _____

a jam and ham sandwich _____

someone who always walks backwards _____

an animal that speaks _____

someone who can fly _____

a pot plant that asks for water when it needs it _Speaking seed_____

Invent three more words with your own definitions.

_____

_____

_____

Puzzle 5

Complete the crossword.

Each of the answers begins with a number prefix.
The clues will help you!

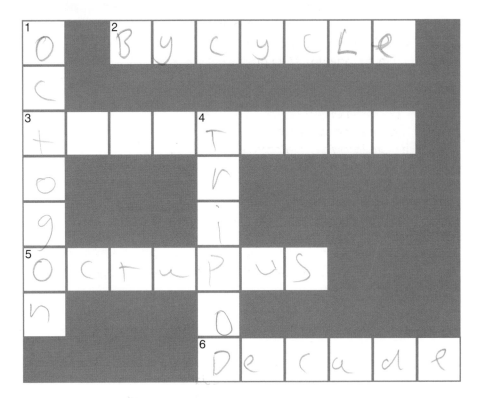

Across

2   A two-wheeled vehicle.

3   A race in three parts.

5   An underwater animal with eight tentacles.

6   Ten years.

Down

1   A shape with eight sides.

4   A stand often used with a camera.

Key words

Some special words are used in this book. You will find them picked out in *italics*. These words are explained here.

abbreviation	a word that has been shortened
adjective	a word that describes somebody or something
adverb	a word that gives extra meaning to a verb
alphabetical order	words arranged in the order of the letters in the alphabet
antonym	a word with a meaning opposite to another word, e.g. hot/cold
clause	a section of a sentence with a verb
comparative	describes the amount of something (adverb or adjective), e.g. more, bigger
compound word	a word made up of two other words, e.g. football
conjunction	a word used to link sentences, phrases or words, e.g. and, but
contraction	two words shortened into one with an apostrophe placed where the letter/s have been dropped, e.g. do not/don't
definition	the meaning of a word
diminutive	a word implying smallness, e.g. duckling
homophone	a word that has the same sound as another but a different meaning or spelling, e.g. right/write
idiom	a phrase that is not meant literally
infinitive	the basic form of the verb, e.g. to scream
metaphor	a figurative expression in which something is described in terms usually associated with something else, e.g. the sky is a sapphire sea
mnemonic	a way of aiding the memory, e.g. a rhyme or silly story
noun	a naming word
abstract noun	a noun referring to a concept or idea, e.g. love, beauty
collective noun	a noun referring to a group or collection of things, e.g. a swarm of bees
common noun	a general name of a person, place or thing, e.g. boy, office
proper noun	the specific name or title of a person or a place, e.g. Ben, London
onomatopoeic	a word that echoes a sound, associated with its meaning, e.g. hiss
phrase	a group of words that do not contain both a subject and a verb
adjectival phrase	a group of words describing a noun
plural	more than one, e.g. cats
prefix	a group of letters added to the beginning of a word, e.g. un, dis
preposition	a word that links nouns and pronouns to other parts of a sentence, e.g. he sat *behind* the door
pronoun	a word that can be used instead of a noun
reported speech	what has been said without using the exact words or speech marks
root word	a word to which a prefix or suffix can be added to make another word, e.g. quick – *quick*ly
simile	an expression to describe what something is like, e.g. as cold as ice
singular	one of something, e.g. cat
suffix	a group of letters added to the end of a word, e.g. ly, ful
superlative	describes the limit of a quality (adjective or adverb), e.g. most, least, shortest
synonym	a word with a very similar meaning to another word, e.g. quick/fast
verb	a 'doing' or 'being' word

Progress Grid

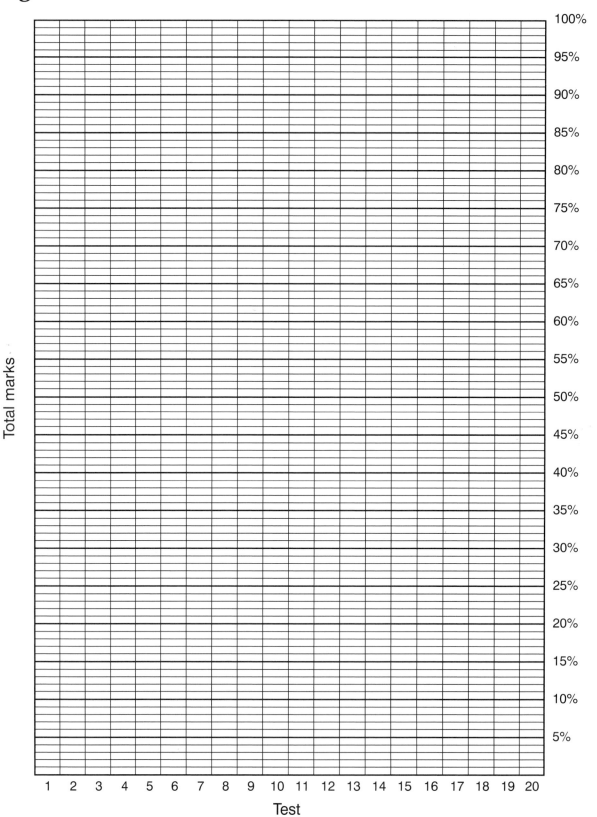

Total marks

100%
95%
90%
85%
80%
75%
70%
65%
60%
55%
50%
45%
40%
35%
30%
25%
20%
15%
10%
5%

1 2 3 4 5 6 7 8 9 10 11 12 13 14 15 16 17 18 19 20

Test